LANCASTER COUNTY ARCHITECTURE

1700-1850

Arthur Armstrong painting c. 1848
of the 1805 Jacob Miller House,
Lancaster Township

LANCASTER COUNTY ARCHITECTURE
1700-1850

Introduction by Gerald S. Lestz

Photographic contributions by John Herr

HISTORIC PRESERVATION TRUST OF LANCASTER COUNTY

Copyright © 1992 by Historic Preservation Trust of Lancaster County
Library of Congress Cataloging in Publication Data
ISBN 0-9635153-0-6
Printed in the United States of America

Designed by Agnew & Corrigan, Inc.
Printed by Intelligencer Printing Company

First Edition

ACKNOWLEDGEMENTS

The Historic Preservation Trust of Lancaster County extends its appreciation
to the following corporations and individuals for their generous
capital or in-kind support to this publication:

Acer/PSC Engineers and Consultants, Inc.

Agnew & Corrigan

Barley, Snyder, Senft & Cohen

Linda Newman Brown, ASID

BURLE INDUSTRIES, INC.

George C. Delp

William W. Durland

John Herr Photography

Intelligencer Printing Company

Lancaster Ultra-Graphics

McMinn's Asphalt Co., Inc.

Penn Savings Bank

Potlatch Corporation

Reese, Lower, Patrick & Scott

Restore 'n' More

Suburban Cable of Lancaster County

Patricia A. Wetzel

White Oak Printing

INTRODUCTION

Lancaster County, Pennsylvania, has an impressive array of eighteenth- and early nineteenth-century family homes and other buildings comprising a rich and varied collection of architecture that is among the choicest in the nation.

The earliest permanent European settlers started with simple temporary shelters, all made by hand with rudimentary tools. Penn's Woods provided materials for the dwellings carved out of the wilderness. The architecture reflects past traditions, the emerging patterns of the times and the personal aspirations of their owners. The buildings which still remain represent a rare treasure for us to admire, study and preserve.

Family annals, neighborhood accounts and community histories preserved information. Interviews and studies of land and tax records have added extension of data that bear on structure histories. Letters and journals give valued aid. Visual documentation on the appearance of individual buildings, properties and townscapes is available in paintings and sketches done by either visiting or local artists from 1757 onward.

The buildings presented in this book typify the cumulative story of the growth of a beloved county — a special place unto itself — and the pride its people take in preserving the best of the past while working for the best in the present and future.

A feeling of permanence pervades. No matter how architectural design has changed since the early 1700s, and no matter how many innovations will be introduced in the future, these old buildings are living monuments providing comfort, stability and aesthetic delight to their occupants. Together, they are a joy to behold. Many are visible from streets and highways, but some are in remote locations, back from the road, screened by huge old trees. Most of the buildings shown in this book are private property, and readers are asked to respect that if they go looking. This is a record book, not a guide book.

William Penn, an English Quaker, was granted the province of Pennsylvania by British monarch Charles II in 1681. A believer in freedom of religion, Penn extended invitations to the persecuted and the poor in many countries. German Mennonites took him at his word, and in 1709 a group of Mennonites under Hans Herr received Penn grants and came to the area that was to become Lancaster County.

Traders and trappers, as well as Native Americans, had coursed through here but formed no settlement. In 1710, these lands on which the Mennonites settled were in a remote part of Chester County. English, Scots-Irish, Welsh, French and other individuals and groups began to arrive. Some early settlers fashioned lean-to shelters, interwoven with brush and saplings, with a sharply sloping roof that kept out the rain and snow. One side of the shelter opened toward a fire used for both heating and cooking.

William Penn, in pamphlets issued to attract settlers, told how to build log cabins:

". . . thirty foot long and eighteen foot broad . . . with a partition near the middle and another to divide one end of the House into two small Rooms . . . with a loft over all . . . The lower floor is the Ground . . . This may seem a mean way of Building but 'tis sufficient and safest for ordinary beginners."

By 1729, when the County of Lancaster was incorporated as the fourth Pennsylvania county, there was a strong nucleus of settlers for formation of an English style of colonial and local governments. The borough charter for the town of Lancaster was granted in 1742.

Franklin Ellis, local nineteenth-century historian, described the inland trek from Philadelphia made by the settlers:

"After arriving at the place selected, which was always convenient to some spring, the covered wagons served as a home for the children and females, while the men and boys put up temporary shelters for themselves until a log cabin could be built . . . The open air was their kitchen . . . Here the meals were prepared and served on a table consisting of the end-gate of the wagon nailed upon the stump of a tree . . .

By the second or third generation, these pioneer families were erecting solid homes of brick, stone or frame. Their barns, of course, had been built as early as possible, and one writer in 1753 said barns were "as large as palaces." Family members — parents and children — were joined by neighbors in the construction of homes and outbuildings. Stone was quarried locally; much was found in the fields, and gathered and assembled over a period of several years, if necessary. Rural homes were often built near strong-running springs.

Dr. Benjamin Rush, famed physician who helped found Franklin and Marshall College, wrote a laudatory essay on the Pennsylvania Germans in 1789, saying of them:

"They always provide large and stable accommodations for their horses and cattle before they lay out much money in building a home for themselves . . . The first dwelling house upon their farms is small and built of logs. It generally lasts the lifetime of the first settler . . . They have a saying, 'A son should always begin his improvements where his father left off'; that is by building a large and convenient stone house."

If the German layout or room plan was followed, a large chimney was placed in the center; if the English or Scots-Irish style prevailed, chimneys graced both gable ends. Datestones in houses and barns were the custom, often high in the gable end. In a salute to womanhood, the husband made certain that his wife's name was with his on the datestone. This seems to have been an early custom peculiar to the Pennsylvania Germans, as examples of it can be seen throughout the county.

Many homes now stand alone, having lost their outbuildings through a variety of causes. But it should be emphasized — and remembered — that the farm house was once surrounded by many structures, of which the barn was the largest. Amos Long, Jr., in his scholarly book, "The Pennsylvania German Family Farm," lists the outbuildings which might flank a farm home. Each had a specific purpose, and not every farm had all.

Those for domestic purposes were clustered closest to the house: tenant house, springhouse, summerhouse, bakeoven, root cellar, malthouse-stillhouse, distillery, smokehouse, woodshed, privy, washhouse, pump house, butcherhouse, cold frames and hot beds. Others, for farming, comprised the hay barrick-hay barn, wagonshed-carriage house, toolshed, smithy, pig pen, chickenhouse, sheepfold, corn crib, limekiln, milkhouse, and tobacco barn or shed.

As the farmers were building in the country, residents of the towns and villages were erecting homes and business places. On the main streets, dwellings went up, often containing the shops of the owners — makers of silverware, furniture, rifles and other objects of utility or beauty. A variety of outbuildings was constructed around town homes as well.

Travelers and other writers wrote on observations of farmhouses and the overall picture of buildings in Lancaster County. One of the first to write on these subjects was Lieutenant Thomas Anburey, a British officer who was here while a prisoner of war during the Revolution. He wrote in a letter dated December 16, 1778, at Lancaster, of his transfer with others of Burgoyne's former troops from Philadelphia:

"After you get over the Delaware, a new country presents itself, extremely well cultivated and inhabited; the roads are lined with farm houses, some of which are near the road, and some at a little distance, and the space between the road and houses is taken up with fields and meadows; some of them (the homes) are built of stone, two stories high, and covered with cedar shingles, but most of them are wooden, with the crevices stopped with clay; the ovens are commonly built a little distance from the house, and under a roof to secure them against the weather."

ARCHITECTURAL STYLES

Germanic
c. 1710 – 1770

The house known as the Herr House was built by Christian Herr in 1719 as a home for his aging parents, Hans and Elizabeth, but also as a Mennonite meetinghouse. The home was erected on a hill, in a style that could be traced back to the Roman occupation of European lands where Germanic tribes resided.

Christian Herr House
c. 1719

Christian had had an earlier log house, which was razed for the stone building. Stone was found on the site; nearby trees provided timbers. An arched stone cellar was dug under part of the home. The stone central chimney served two fireplaces for cooking and warmth. The roof has a steep pitch to repel snow. The oaken shingles are side-lapped as well as top- and bottom-lapped, following the German style, to give added protection against rain that might enter on the dominant western winds. The stone window frames and casement windows now in the house follow the patterns of the originals. Hardware and glass might have been brought in by the wagons of James Logan, William Penn's secretary, who owned an outpost nearby, or from Philadelphia.

Elsewhere in the county are other homes and buildings which are also in the Germanic-style category: the Cloister in Ephrata, as well as homes in Lititz, Manheim and Lancaster. All have their stylistic roots in the medieval ancestral homes.

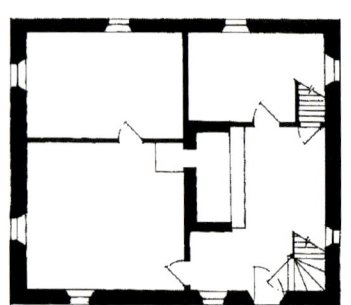

Germanic Floorplan

Central chimney, small and unbalanced window openings.

Traditional English
c. 1710 – 1770

Among the earliest English settlers of Lancaster County was the Wright family who hailed from Lancaster, England, which in bygone days had been a Roman camp. John Wright, born about 1667, was one of the first to build a home, and gave the county its name for his home shire. The town was first known as Wright's Ferry, but the name was changed to Columbia during the unsuccessful effort to win selection of the village as the site of the nation's capital.

Wright's Ferry Mansion
c. 1738

The Wright's Ferry Mansion was erected in 1738 by Susannah Wright, born in 1697. She was an exceptional person who chose the style — Traditional English — harking back to medieval times. Long and narrow, the home contains paneling in the later Georgian style, probably added after it was occupied.

This mansion of gray stone, one room deep, with 12 over 12 window panes on the first floor and 9 over 9 on the second, is one that a visitor to Lancaster, England, might see there today. It typifies two characteristics which should be noted in any study of Lancaster County architecture.

The first is a melding of traditions. Even though its owner was of English stock and envisioned a home she and her family might have occupied had they not traveled to North America, German workmen must have been among those hired to build the home. Today's scholars credit the Germanic influence for the long wooden shingles, the squirrel tail oven, and the pent roof which extends out over the first floor windows. This merging of

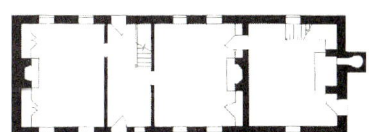

Traditional English Floorplan

Long, narrow, one room-deep, with gable-end chimneys.

traditions also occurred in other homes of the period and later.

The second element is permanence. While the sources of design were medieval or earlier, the home did continue to afford a dwelling place for well over 250 years. Homes throughout Lancaster County were built to last. Their beauty and craftsmanship are very evident.

Georgian
c. 1730 – 1795

Georgian architecture takes its name from the three kings, George I, II and III, who ruled Britain from 1714 to 1820. English immigrants to Penn's and other colonies had seen Georgian-style homes and larger buildings before they boarded ship to sail the Atlantic; in some cases they also had design books to use as guides.

Georgian was more ornate than its predecessor styles. Homes were usually brick or stone, two or three stories high. The placement of doors and windows was often symmetrical. Bricks were typically laid in Flemish bond — alternate long bricks and short (also known as "headers"). Under the second story window of brick structures, a double line of brick often projected out in what was called the belt line or course. Under the first story windows was the water table, extending a few inches from the main wall and deflecting rain or snow from the foundations.

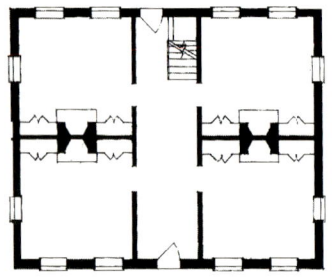

Georgian Floorplan

Internal and external symmetry, with central entryway.

Rock Ford
c. 1795

Other Georgian features, not all on one house but found in various parts of the county, included: central keystones over windows; pedimented doorways; double-hung 12 over 12 windows on the first floor, with 8 over 12 above; porches, also known as piazzas; and cornices with dentils.

Examples of Georgian homes in Lancaster City are the Sehner-Ellicott-von Hess House, now headquarters of the Historic Preservation Trust; Rock Ford, home of General Edward Hand; the John Messencope home; and the Neff-Passmore House, all constructed of brick.

Georgian homes can be found throughout Lancaster County. Some Georgian structures in other places, notably Philadelphia, were more grandiose in character. Lancaster Countians would have seen some of those either on the way here or on visits later, but Lancaster's homes reflected a restrained, elegant conservatism that was an early hallmark of local character. Germanic influences are frequently evident, including encircling pent roof between the first and second floors, gable end pent eaves, and quoins. Let it be noted that the buildings were not drawn by architects; people did not call themselves that here. There were builders, however, familiar with Georgian style.

William Penn, a Quaker, drew many of his co-religionists to Lancaster County, particularly to the eastern and southern sectors. Design for Quaker homes was the ultimate in simplicity, with no ornamentation. Some authorities call it a three-room cottage, or a two-thirds Georgian because of its lesser size. Often the front doorway was not centered because there was no central hallway. Instead it was located to the left or right, and two windows completed the design. This was in contrast to the balanced design of traditional Georgian architecture.

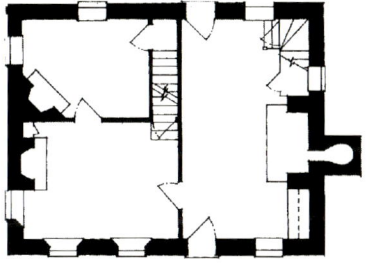

Quaker Floorplan

Typical 3-room plan with entry into kitchen.

Meetinghouses built by the Quakers survive. One is at Penn Hill, in Wakefield. A larger meetinghouse east of Christiana, the Sadsbury, is squared, more Traditional English than specifically Quaker.

Federal
c. 1790 – 1830

The term "Federal" came into popular use in the United States after the Constitution was adopted in 1789, as an expression of pride in the new nation. In architecture, it was applied to what might be called the first American style, which typified the desire for change toward a new national identity won in armed conflict. Federal architecture was popular in Lancaster County from the late eighteenth century through the 1830s. This was a time of significant growth and prosperity.

Different characteristics of Federal architecture are arches with fanlights over doors; absence of water tables and belt course; six over six window sash; oval, elliptical or circular forms; delicate ornament; paneled shutters on the first floor and slatted shutters (usually green) on the second floor; thin, light moldings; and gabel-end chimney.

Wheatland, home of President James Buchanan, is one of the most famous local Federal-style houses, albeit from 1828, late in the style period. Quite often, Georgian details were included in Federal-style homes.

Wheatland
c. 1828

Federal floorplans are similar to Georgian floorplans with the long side facing the street and the entrance in the center when freestanding. In many urban settings, the buildings are in a row with the short side facing the street and the entrance on one side of the facade. Larger, more elaborate Federal houses often have flanking wings.

Classical Revival
c. 1820 – 1850

The term Classical Revival refers to the art and design interest spurred by the renewed reverence shown in the early and middle 1800s to the styles of ancient Rome or Greece. New England displayed widespread zeal for Classical Revival and so did Philadelphia, but few examples exist in Lancaster County.

The Grubb Mansion in Lancaster City is one of the best Greek Revival homes in the county. Another superb example is the Leaman Mansion in Paradise Township, built in the 1830s by a bridegroom who had seen homes like it on his honeymoon along the Hudson.

Stylistic elements of Classical Revival include monumental, pedimented portico with tall columns, post and lintel type designs for doorways, transoms and fanlights at principal doorways, six over six window sash, heavy moldings, and gable-end entrances.

Over the years, styles have blended. Many homeowners have added porches or porticos with tall columns to the fronts of homes that originally had none, to create an effect of Classical Revival. One of the best examples is the Donegal Mills plantation.

Donegal Mills Plantation
c. 1830 portico

Further information and examples of later architecture not included in this volume are available from the Historic Preservation Trust of Lancaster County. Lancaster County's stewardship of the land extends to architecture. The photographs that follow give ample testimony that such stewardship is in active practice. It is the purpose of this book to heighten awareness of Lancaster County's rich architectural heritage and to extend its preservation to future generations.

Christian Herr House
West Lampeter Township
c. 1719
Also known as the Hans Herr House. A fine example of early Germanic domestic architecture. The date is carved into the stone lintel over the door.

Rear view of the Christian Herr House.

Martin Mylin Gun Shop
West Lampeter Township
c. 1719
The other side of the shop has large barn-like double doors.

Abraham Herr Farmstead
Lancaster Township
c. 1725
The steeply pitched roof of this home is characteristic of early Germanic architecture.

Mennonite Meetinghouse
East Hempfield Township
c. 1730
This whitewashed Germanic log building has gable-end pent eave and batten shutters.

Robert Fulton Birthplace
Fulton Township
c. 1734
Robert Fulton, "father of the steamboat," was born in this home in 1765.

Ephrata Cloister
Ephrata Borough
c. 1733, 1741, 1743, 1760
The Saal, or meetinghouse,
and kitchen wing.

21

A workroom in the Saron,
or Sisters' House.

Theadorus Eby House
Earl Township
c. 1735
This Germanic farmhouse had
a central chimney.

Kauffman Distillery
Manor Township
c. 1740
Early still house or distillery, on the Kauffman farm.

Wright's Ferry Mansion
Columbia Borough
c. 1738
This home of Susannah Wright has a Traditional English floorplan, pent eave and squirrel tail oven.

Martin Weybrecht House
Manheim Township
c. 1741
Early farmhouse with segmented arch windows on first floor. Window sash are later replacements.

Donegal Presbyterian Church
Donegal Township
c. 1740
The gambrel roof of this church shows the Irish influence of the congregation.

West Lampeter Township
c. 1740
Early stone house across from
the Christian Herr House.

Byerland Church
Pequea Township
c. 1747
One of the earliest Mennonite churches known to exist in the United States. The back fireplace wall of this building is stone.

28

John Musser House
Manor Township
c. 1744, 1800
This house was built in two sections. Central chimney, segmented stone arches and quoins are characteristics of Germanic architecture.

William Downing House
Bart Township
c. 1747
Known as Bartshire, this home is an excellent example
of Traditional English architectural features such as
one-room-deep plan and gable-end chimneys.

Strasburg Borough
c. 1757
The gable end of this 1-1/2 story
home is of half-timber construction.

LANCASTER COUNTY

32

33

Pennock Mill
Drumore Township
c. 1750
The site of various mill operations, the mill is known locally as Pennock Mill, after Simon Pennock, who owned the mill in the early 1800s.

35

Windsor Forge Mansion
Caernarvon Township
c. 1750, 1815
English-style forge complex of buildings including mansion house with gambrel roof, summer kitchen, smokehouse, springhouse and tenant houses.

Michael Shenk House
Elizabeth Township
c. 1750
This Germanic-style home features wooden cornice and gable-end pent eave.

Martin Farm Springhouse
Earl Township
c. 1750
Early houses were often built near strong-running springs.

Frederick White House
Paradise Township
c. 1750
Germanic farmhouse with Huguenot influences such as double-pegged frames. The log house addition was moved from a nearby site.

Michael Whitmore House
Manor Township
c. 1752
This home shows an early blending of English and Germanic influences.

Peter I. Stauffer House
East Earl Township
c. 1752
This stone home has an unusual frame addition.

Philip Ferree, Sr. House
Leacock Township
c. 1754, 1794
The earliest portion of this home was built in 1725. Seventeenth-century coins found under the floorboards suggest the original use as a tavern.

Lewis Cassler House
Known as Warden's House
Lititz Borough
c. 1757
One of the original buildings of the Moravian settlement exhibiting high-style Germanic features.

Benedict Eschleman House
Manor Township
c. 1759
This early home has a surviving plaster cove cornice and ornate datestones. Window sash have been replaced and encircling pent roof removed.

"Benedict Eschleman and his housewife, Anna, have built this home in the year 1759"

Valentine Stover House
Known as the Checkerboard House
Elizabeth Township
c. 1760
Cut stones in alternating shades
create a bold and distinctive look.

Isaac Long Farmstead
Manheim Township
c. 1760
This Germanic-style farmhouse had a red tile roof.

Robert King House
Drumore Township
c. 1760, 1819
Stone bankhouse with early nineteenth-century addition.

Messencope-Demuth House
Lancaster City
c. 1760
This house retains the only original plastered cove cornice in
the city. Charles Demuth, Lancaster's most noted twentieth-century
painter, lived here.

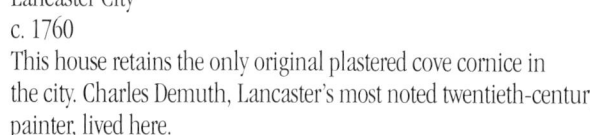

William Bausman House
Lancaster City
c. 1761

The "eavesdropper" carved into the cornice is an unusual feature of this city building.

Muhlenberg House
Lancaster City
c. 1760
Early 2-1/2 story city house.

Old Sadsbury Friends' Meetinghouse
Sadsbury Township
c. 1760
One of the oldest surviving Quaker meetinghouses in Lancaster County. The two-story height and low-pitched hip roof are atypical of meetinghouses in the county.

Manheim Borough
c. 1762
This limestone house has brick
segmented arches and 12 over 8 window sash
on the first floor. Datestones have been removed.

Werner House
Lititz Borough
c. 1762
Early 1-1/2 story frame village house.

The door transom, shutters, 6 over 6 sash and the dormers are Federal-style alterations, stylistically dating between 1815 and 1835.

Mohler Farmstead
Ephrata Township
c. 1764
Early Germanic sandstone house
with center chimney.

Benedick Eschelman House
Conestoga Township
c. 1764
This house survives with many period outbuildings. The current porch, or piazza, and double doors are later additions.

Abraham Landis House
East Lampeter Township
c. 1763
This stone house with symmetrical Georgian facade has restored pents and bake oven.

Jacob Fouts House
Strasburg Borough
c. 1764
Germanic house with central chimney and evidence of a missing pent eave on the front facade.

Caushey-Ankrim House
Drumore Township
c. 1765, 1780
The original section of this house has a slate gable-end datestone. The other half mimics the original and dates 1780-1815. An outdoor bake oven also survives.

57

Christian Stauffer House
East Lampeter Township
c. 1767
A rare raised plasterwork inscription in the entry hall ceiling bears the date and the initials CST. The frame section is a mid-nineteenth century addition.

The parlor also retains a raised plasterwork ceiling medallion. Evidence in the plaster provided the outlines for reproducing the benches lining the walls and the "holy corner" shelf.

Stubbs-Cutler House
Drumore Township
c. 1767, 1830
A three-part English floorplan house, barn and reconstructed smokehouse remain on this farm complex. The two stone additions to the house pre-date 1830.

Andres Graeff House
Lancaster Township
c. 1767
Paired datestones flank the center, second-story window of this restored classic Georgian house with encircling pent roof.

61

Jacob Hostetter House
Manor Township
c. 1769
The four-bay limestone section of this house has sandstone arches over the first-floor windows.

Daniel Bauman House
Ephrata Borough
c. 1769
The central chimney, gable-end pent eave and stone arches over the windows are Germanic features.

Oberholtzer House
East Petersburg Borough
c. 1769
The porch on this house is believed to be original. Double second-floor datestones adorn the front facade.

John Douglass House
Colerain Township
c. 1769
Early stone house with gable-end pent eave and segmented arches over windows.

A rare eighteenth-century log outhouse survives behind the house.

Nicholas Hollinger Barn
Conoy Township
c. 1770
One of a very few log barns still remaining in Lancaster County.

Andrew Kauffman Mill
Manor Township
c. 1770
"Erbaut Von Andreas Kauffman und Veronica Kauffman Anno 1770" reads the datestone of this stone mill. It is now a residence.

Reiber-Herr-Hershey House
Manor Township
c. 1772
Germanic-style house with traditional three-room plan and central chimney. A spring runs through the basement.

Benedick Eschelman House
Strasburg Township
c. 1770
The window sash and porch are later additions. Originally a pent roof would have encircled the house between the first and second floors.

BENEDICK
ESCHELMAN
ANNA. E. M
~ 1770 ~

Johannes Harnish House
West Lampeter Township
c. 1774
The basement entry has a segmented keystone arch.

Jasper Yeates House
Salisbury Township
c. 1775, 1795
This house marks the development of a new vernacular farmhouse type, varying from the strict symmetry of the Georgian style. The porch dates from the 1795 addition and renovations completed for Jasper Yeates.

McCullough House
East Drumore Township
c. 1775, 1800
Striking for its simplicity of form and lack of later additions, this Georgian-style house, built in two parts, has original window sash and gable-end pent eave.

Fasig House
Manheim Borough
c. 1775
The Manheim Historical Society's building is typical of early Germanic log houses in Manheim Borough. It was relocated to this site in 1974.

John Jenkins Jr. House
Caernarvon Township
c. 1775
The stone section of this house is of traditional Georgian style with symmetrical door and window placement, multi-paned double-hung sash and cornice dentil details.

Manheim Borough
c. 1775
Early log home with clapboard siding. Once common, few buildings of this type remain.

Hopewell Forge Mansion
Elizabeth Township
c. 1775
The four-bay facade with entrance on the end bay is atypical of the Georgian style.

Compass Mill
Also known as Rome Mill
Warwick Township
c. 1776
The high-pitched roof and chevron-patterned doors are Germanic features of this mill.

Pool Forge
Caernarvon Township
c. 1779
The earliest portion of this ironmaster's mansion was built pre-1780.

Paymaster's Building
Pool Forge
c. 1790-1815
The Paymaster's Building at Pool Forge was built in the late eighteenth century.

Kinsey Farmstead
Mount Joy Township
c. 1780-1820
Vernacular, early log farmstead with addition.

Stone-end barn on the Kinsey Farm has massive quoins.

Dr. Christian Neff House
Also known as Neff-Passmore House
Lancaster City
c. 1785
This structure bears many of the characteristics of the classic Georgian style. Sometime after its construction, it was owned by John Passmore, Lancaster City's first mayor.

Lynche House
Lancaster City
c. 1775, 1830
This house is notable for its half-timber gable end. The lower story was altered in the first half of the nineteenth century.

Michael Musser House
Lancaster City
c. 1785

Georgian-style house with fine pedimented doorway. The Marquis de Lafayette stayed here when he returned to America in 1825.

81

Sehner-Ellicott-von Hess House
Built by Gottlieb Sehner
Lancaster City
c. 1789
Georgian-style house with
three-bay facade, central chimney
and keystones over the windows.
Home of noted surveyor
Andrew Ellicott.

Andrew Kauffman House
Manor Township
c. 1785
Bank farmhouse built by Andrew Kauffman. A spring runs through the basement.

Shenk Barn
Conestoga Township
c. 1786
Stone barn with pierced gable ends.

Michael Baughman House
East Hempfield Township
c. 1790
Formal Georgian-style house
with keystones over the windows.

Ewing-Hershey House
East Donegal Township
c. 1790
Portions of this four-bay limestone house may date into the mid-eighteenth century.

White Swan Tavern
Marietta Borough
c. 1790, 1815
This building was long used as an inn and tavern.
Clapboard-sided structures were once very common.
The oldest portion of the inn dates from 1768.

Boehm's Methodist Church
Pequea Township
c. 1791
This stone church was recently restored
to its eighteenth-century appearance.

Spring Grove Forge Mansion
Built by Cyrus Jacobs
East Earl Township
c. 1790, 1805

89

The main facade of this 2-1/2 story Georgian-style home was built in two sections. The right section was built in 1790.

Johannes Mueller House
Lititz Borough
c. 1792
Germanic-style 1-1/2 story stone house. The log addition on the end was built in 1794.

Window and door detail of the Mueller House.

Trinity Lutheran Church
Lancaster City
c. 1766, 1794
This familiar steeple has graced Lancaster's skyline since 1794. The main Georgian structure was constructed in 1766.

Old Town Hall
Lancaster City
c. 1795
Large Georgian building with window keystones, belt course, water table and pedimented door. The third floor was added in the 1830s.

Jacob Kimmell House
Ephrata Borough
c. 1795
Georgian sandstone house with
12 over 12 windows and keystones.

East Hempfield Township
c. 1795
Early 1-1/2 story village house.

Gen. Edward Hand House
Rock Ford
Lancaster Township
c. 1795
Fine Georgian home built by Edward Hand, George Washington's adjutant general.

Greiner House
Mount Joy Township
c. 1795
This sandstone house is unique for its early use of a gable-end entry. The gable pent eave, flat cut-stone arches with keystones and use of 8 over 8 window sash are typical elements of this period.

Johan Mohler House
Ephrata Township
c. 1794
This Georgian house is largely intact, having most of its original exterior and interior woodwork.

Philip Friedrich House
Warwick Township
c. 1797
Georgian-style house with 12 over 12 windows on the first floor and 12 over 8 windows on the second floor. Interior woodwork shows Federal influences.

99

Peter Lefever House
Strasburg Township
c. 1797, 1821
Eighteenth-century stone house with nineteenth-century brick addition. Both sections have datestones. Brick and stone smokehouse is located next to the house.

John Haldeman Mansion
Conoy Township
Pre-1798, 1812
Also known as Locust Grove, this house has been undergoing restoration of the exterior to appear as it would have in the early 1800s. It exhibits features of both the Georgian and Federal styles.

101

John Showalter House
Earl Township
c. 1799
A wooden date tablet is found in the
second-floor facade wall of this home.

New Holland Reformed Church
New Holland Borough
c. 1799
This is one of the most elegant meetinghouse-type churches in Lancaster County.

John Pfeiffer House
Manheim Township
c. 1799
This Georgian-style farmhouse has a pedimented front doorway
similar to the Sehner-Ellicott-von Hess House in Lancaster City.
Window sash have been replaced.

Christian Nolt House
West Hempfield Township
c. 1799
Early stone farmhouse with later window sash.

Old County Hospital
Lancaster City
c. 1799
Early hospital featuring flat-arch brick lintels and end chimney on the west facade.

David Jamison House
West Donegal Township
c. 1800
This complex of buildings includes a brick mansion house, 1-1/2 story brick and stone house, barn and stone springhouse.

Springhouse
East Drumore Township
c. 1800
Intact early rural springhouse.

Abraham and Christian Herr House
Lancaster Township
c. 1800
This house is located directly across from the 1725 Abraham Herr House.

John Shenk Farm *[bottom]*
Manor Township
c. 1800
Early stone farmhouse with a series of additions that occurred over time.

Wendell Hibschman House
Ephrata Township
c. 1801, 1803
Georgian-style farmhouse
with 12 over 12 window sash.

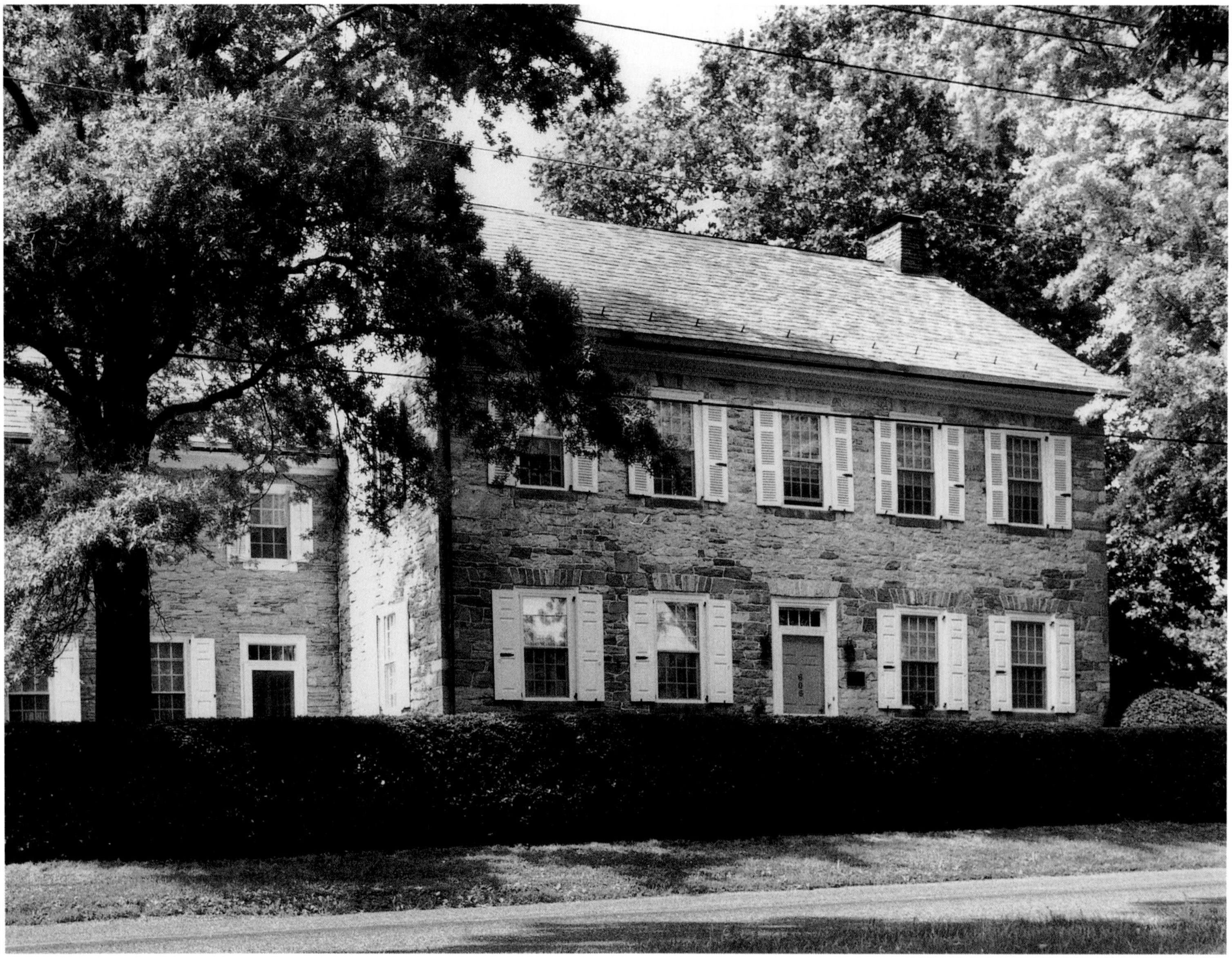

Large stone barn with
arched doorway.

Hunsecker Barn
Mount Joy Township
c. 1800
Typical Pennsylvania stone bankbarn.

Eastland Friends' Meetinghouse
Little Britain Township
c. 1803
Quaker-style stone meetinghouse
with carriage shed in the foreground.

Timothy Haines House
Fulton Township
c. 1804
This Federal-style farmhouse is part of a complex including barns and other outbuildings.

Christopher Brenner House
Known as Abbeville
Lancaster Township
c. 1805
This Georgian-style house, with additions, has Federal and Classical Revival characteristics.

Peter Lindemuth House
Rapho Township
c. 1805
Limestone house with end chimneys and 9 over 9 windows.

Swamp Reformed Church
West Cocalico Township
c. 1806
This sandstone church was designed with lighter color quoins, sills and keystone lintels.

Slaymaker House
Known as White Chimneys
Salisbury Township
c. 1807
Rear portion of this house was built as a tavern in 1720.

Peter Elser House
Clay Township
c. 1807
This Federal-style house was built by a prosperous miller and farmer.

Ann Shay Evans House
Caernarvon Township
c. 1808
Sandstone house with prominent keystones over all windows.

East Hempfield Township
c. 1808
Symmetrical limestone house
with arched central doorway, quoins
and missing piazza.

Michael Siegrist House
West Hempfield Township
c. 1809
Georgian-style farmstead with later window sash. The stone flashing course indicates the presence of an original piazza.

Nissley House
Rapho Township
c. 1811
This farmhouse has a seven-bay facade with
Federal-style woodwork of exceptional quality. The
frame structure in the foreground is a summer kitchen.

Fountain Tavern
Built by George Snyder
West Hempfield Township
c. 1808
This Federal-style tavern has prominent arched, paired central doorways.

Miller's House
c. 1810
This small stone house was the
residence of the miller.

125

Windom Mill
Built by Jacob Kauffman
Manor Township
c. 1810
Part of a very large complex of stone buildings.

Mount Vernon Furnace Mansion
Built by Henry Grubb
West Donegal Township
c. 1811
This Federal-style mansion was the manager's
house and part-time residence of ironmaster Henry Grubb.

Marietta Borough
c. 1811
Federal-style house with "H" chimneys and gable-end fanlight.

Federal-style dormers and "green" shutters are typical.

Risser House
Mount Joy Township
c. 1811
This farmstead features dressed brownstone and gable-end pent eave.

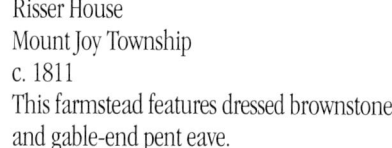

129

Rapho Township
c. 1810
Federal-style house with
elaborate entryway woodwork
and refined fanlight.

Henry Hertzler House
Rapho Township
c. 1813
This large limestone house has paneled first-floor shutters and double doors.

131

The first-floor facade is stuccoed and whitewashed. Double doors and paired datestones, one in German and one in English, are interesting features of this home.

Jacob Mayer House
Manheim Township
c. 1815
This 1-1/2 story home is of log and frame construction.

133

John Pfautz House
Warwick Township
c. 1813
Federal-style farmhouse with paired
German datestones and houseblessing.

The church's original "U" shaped balcony remains intact.

135

Old Zion Reformed Church
Elizabeth Township
c. 1813
This Federal-style church has arched windows and doors with brick segmented arches and keystones.

John Keller House
Ephrata Township
c. 1813
Federal-style farmstead
with a period-style piazza.

Joseph Charles House
Manor Township
c. 1814
Federal-style house with "H" chimney and fanlight on gable end. The entrance in the end bay is atypical.

Jacob Kirk Mansion
Little Britain Township
c. 1815
Five-bay, Federal-style bankhouse
with central entryway.

Dr. Isaac Winters House
Earl Township
c. 1815
Federal-style house constructed of limestone.

John Kurtz House
Ephrata Borough
c. 1815
John Kurtz was a prosperous Amish farmer. The pent eave on front facade is not original.

Long House
Drumore Township
c. 1815
The stone shop near the house
was used to manufacture sickles.

Smokehouse
Built by Jacob Gamber
West Hempfield Township
c. 1815
Somewhat intact stone smokehouse stands alone today.

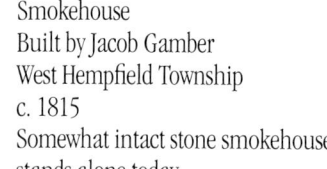

143

Bear House
West Cocalico Township
c. 1815
Federal-style house constructed of limestone with sandstone quoins.

Drumore Friends' Meetinghouse
Drumore Township
c. 1816
Stuccoed stone meetinghouse belonging to the Hicksite Branch of the Quakers.

St. Michael's Lutheran Church
Strasburg Borough
c. 1816
This Georgian-style church has Federal influences such as arched windows. The steeple planned for the east gable end was never completed.

Brick Barn
Rapho Township
c. 1816
This bankbarn has pierced or reticulated brickwork designed into the gable ends for circulation.

Jacob Getz House
East Hempfield Township
c. 1818
Federal-style farmhouse with
arched double entrances.

This rather plain Federal-style meetinghouse
has arched doorways with fanlights.

149

Union Meetinghouse
Marietta Borough
c. 1818

Manor Township
c. 1818
This Federal-style house has elaborate doorways with arched fanlights.

Foxfire House
Clay Township
c. 1820
Sandstone bankhouse with adjacent bake oven.

Fredrick Clear House
West Hempfield Township
c. 1820
Short windows on the second story of this house are an unusual feature.

Michael Gross House
West Donegal Township
Mansion c. 1819
Small House c. 1790
This Federal-style mansion with addition has a center hallway and elliptical stairway rising from the first floor to the attic.

Hershey Mill House
Manor Township
c. 1820
This stone house is said to have been
built after construction of the mill.

Hershey Mill
Manor Township
c. 1810
This well-preserved stone mill stands across from the Mill House.

Kirk-Haines House
Little Britain Township
c. 1820
This Quaker-style, Federal farmhouse is stuccoed and whitewashed.

Jacob Keller House
Ephrata Township
c. 1820
Federal-style stone bankhouse built over a spring.

Penn Hill Friends' Meetinghouse
Fulton Township
c. 1823
This understated Federal-style meetinghouse has quarter-round windows on the gable end.

George Haverstick House
Pequea Township
c. 1825
This brick bankhouse with gable-end chimneys has a recent log addition.

Lancaster City
c. 1825
Federal-style brick bankhouse has an overhanging roof that created a prominent second-floor piazza.

Cyrus Jacobs House
Known as Wheatland
Caernarvon Township
c. 1825
This mansion has Classical Revival and Federal-style design elements.

Bart Friends' Meetinghouse
Sadsbury Township
c. 1825
The front piazza on this meetinghouse is supported by Classical Revival columns.

Jacob Eichholtz House
Lancaster City
c. 1825
Federal-style home of celebrated portrait painter Jacob Eichholtz.

Wheatland
Built by William Jenkins
Home of President Buchanan
Lancaster Township
c. 1828
Rear view of this Federal-style mansion.

Known as the Shriner Farmstead
Manheim Township
c. 1828
This stone house is part of a farm complex consisting of summer kitchen, stone barn and other outbuildings.

Shriner Barn
Manheim Township
c. 1828
Stone barn with datestone and gable-end arched window.

Marietta Borough
c. 1830
Federal-style home with 8-light transom over the front door.

Nathaniel Ellmaker House
Salisbury Township
c. 1830
This late Federal-style house has Tuscan-order columns at the entryway.

Adam Beery Farmstead
Clay Township
c. 1830
Sandstone bankhouse with quoins.

John Nolt House
West Hempfield Township
c. 1833
Two matched tablets adorn the second-story facade of this Federal-style bankhouse.

Johannes Frantz House
Manor Township
c. 1835
Double front doors are found throughout the county from c. 1815 well into the early 20th century.

Lewis Urban House
Manor Township
c. 1835
This Classical Revival home has a two-story portico supported by Ionic-order columns.

Joseph Good House
Pequea Township
c. 1836
Stone four bay farmhouse with adjacent stone springhouse.

Ephrata Academy
Ephrata Borough
c. 1837
This frame building was constructed by
the Seventh Day German Baptist Church.

John Leaman House
Paradise Township
c. 1839
Classical Revival house built by Dr. Leaman for his bride. The gable-end entrance, Tucsan-columned portico and Palladian window in the gable are characteristics of this style.

George Hauck House
Manheim Township
c. 1842

Clement Grubb House
Lancaster City
c. 1845
This Classical Revival mansion was built by wealthy ironmaster Clement Grubb.

BIBLIOGRAPHY
and suggested reading

Harnish-Baumgardner Mill
Built by Jacob Smith
Pequea Township
c. 1800
Covered bridge c. 1860

Ellis, Franklin and Samuel Evans. *History of Lancaster County*.
Philadelphia: Everts & Peck, 1883.

Fletcher, Stevenson Whitcomb. *Pennsylvania Architecture and Country Life 1640-1840*.
Harrisburg, Pa.: Pennsylvania Historical and Museum Commission, 1950.

Friesen, Steve. *A Modest Mennonite Home*. Intercourse, Pa.: Good Books, 1990.

Gowans, Alan. *Style and Types of North American Architecture*.
New York: Harper Collins, 1992.

Historic Preservation Trust of Lancaster County.
Handbook of Lancaster County Architecture – Styles and Terms. Lancaster, Pa.:
Historic Preservation Trust of Lancaster County, 1979.

_____. *Lancaster Architecture 1719-1927*. Lancaster, Pa.:
Historic Preservation Trust of Lancaster County, 1979.

_____. *Our Present Past*. Lancaster, Pa.:
Historic Preservation Trust of Lancaster County, 1985.

Kauffman, Henry J. *Architecture of the Pennsylvania Dutch Country, 1700-1900*.
Lancaster, Pa.: privately printed, 1992.

Noble, Allen G. *Wood, Brick and Stone*. Boston: University of Massachusetts Press, 1984.

Rush, Benjamin. *An Account of the Manners of the German Inhabitants of Pennsylvania 1789*.
Philadelphia: S.T. Town, 1875.

Stevens, S.K. *Pennsylvania, Birthplace of a Nation*. New York: Random House, 1964.

Worner, William F. *Old Lancaster*. Lancaster, Pa.: privately printed, 1927.